Ten Cats Have Hats

Ten Cats Have Hats

A Counting Book

by Jean Marzollo
Illustrated by David McPhail

HARCOURT BRACE & COMPANY

Orlando Atlanta Austin Boston San Francisco Chicago Dallas New York
Toronto London

For Frank Hodge
—J.M.

For Ben—
"You can't throw the ball by me."
—D.M.

This edition is published by special arrangement with Scholastic Inc.

Grateful acknowledgment is made to Scholastic Inc. for permission to reprint *Ten Cats Have Hats* by Jean Marzollo, illustrated by David McPhail. Text copyright © 1994 by Jean Marzollo; illustrations copyright © 1994 by David McPhail.

Printed in the United States of America

ISBN 0-15-310845-2

2 3 4 5 6 7 8 9 10   026   2002 2001 2000 99

1 One bear has a chair,
but I have a hat.

Two ducks have trucks,
but I have a hat.

Three trees have bees,
but I have a hat.

4 Four stores have doors,
but I have a hat.

5

Five pigs have wigs,
but I have a hat.

6

Six bugs have rugs,
but I have a hat.

Seven goats have coats,

but I have a hat.

8

Eight crabs have cabs,
but I have a hat.

9 Nine snails have trails,
but I have a hat.

Ten cats have hats . . .

just like me.